THE POWER OF BODY LANGUAGE

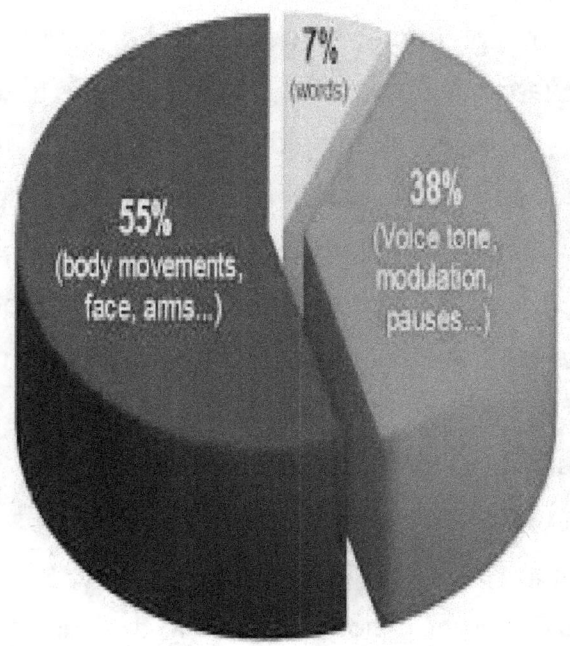

THE IMPORTANCE OF BODY LANGUAGE AND HOW TO USE IT EFFECTIVELY

NOTES TO READER

Table of Contents

INTRODUCTION

Wherever you may travel or take pleasure in you will delight in the sights, sounds, and entertainment of the people and things around you. Most of what you hear and see involve some form of communication and more than likely the majority of that communication is verbal.

With people being so engrossed and involved in their fast paced lives today, it is common for the nonverbal communication to go unnoticed. I mean really, given the world today, people just don't have the time to harp on things that are not spoken. This is a huge mistake, and people can actually miss out on purpose a whole message by not being aware of the nonverbal messages that are being enacted during a conversation. The body movements are communicated through posture, facial expressions, hand gestures, and even eye contact.

Whatever is going on internally with a person usually is displayed on the outside. You ever saw a movie where the actor was being interrogated by a police officer, and they get so nervous that they start stuttering or their eyeballs wonder aimlessly around the person that they are talking to?

Or better yet, nervous beads of sweat just start flowing down their face, and their feet get to tapping uncontrollably? These are sure signs that the person is extremely uneasy and lying because they are hiding important information. How about the girl who overuses her hands when she is attempting to describe a "juicy" situation? You can tell that she's excited to spill the tea and can't talk fast enough to get the gossip out. It's cute and annoying at the same darn time, but she just can't help it.

Having the ability to read people and their gestures put you in a better advantage to communicate better with them and hence, we can learn more about ourselves and become more aware of the nonverbal messages that we are relaying to them. There are also times when we can send the wrong message to people or mixed messages. That's where you say one thing, but your body language is saying the complete opposite or vice versa. You may do this subconsciously or consciously just to trip people up. It's so very important to make sure that your verbal communication matches your nonverbal communication especially in places where you are an authoritative figure or in a professional setting, you want to gain credibility and being "wishy-washy" simply wouldn't be good for business or the development of it.

With the skills, you learn in this book you will become the best human lie detector there ever was, and you will have learned how to exude more confidence and assurance of yourself. You will not only learn how to read the human body but take pride in knowing how to listen to it, as well.

CHAPTER 1: WHAT EXACTLY IS BODY LANGUAGE?

Body language is a kind of non-verbal correspondence in which physical conduct, instead of words, are utilized to express or pass on data. Such conduct incorporates outward appearances, body act, motions, eye development, touch and the utilization of space. Body language exists in both creatures and people; however, this article concentrates on translations of Human Body language. It is otherwise called kinetics.

Body language must not be mistaken for gesture-based communication, as a gesture- based communication is a full dialect and has its own particular complex sentence structure frameworks, and it also has the capacity to show the essential properties that exist in all dialects. Body language, then again, does not have a linguistic use and should be translated extensively, rather than having an outright significance relating to a specific development. So it is not a dialect-like gesture-based communication and is essentially named as a "dialect" because of mainstream culture.

In a group, there are tons of specific conduct. Understandings may differ from nation to nation, or culture to culture. On this note, there is contention on whether body language is general. Body language, a subset of nonverbal correspondence, supplements verbal correspondence in social cooperation. Indeed a few specialists infer that nonverbal correspondence represents the larger part of data transmitted amid interpersonal cooperation. It sets up the relationship between two individuals and directs collaboration, yet can be vague. Subsequently, it is urgent to precisely read body language to abstain from a misconception in social situations.

CHAPTER 2: THE PIONEERS OF BODY LANGUAGE

The art of body language is something that began to gain worldwide traction and genuine interest of notable researchers around the early 20th century. Although there is said to be innovators who have studied this topic long before this century. Francis Bacon happened to be one of the pioneers who took a keen interest in the research of observational body language. This type of research is solely dependent upon observation and experiences as opposed to ideology or thesis. Bacon was an English theorist who happened to be a legislator and scientist, as well, who felt as if the gestures of the body were an extremely important element that had been neglected in research by prior philosophers.

Bacon was adamant that the outward gestures, hence, body language and the demeanor of an individual directly links to the state of mind of that individual. He indicated that the way a person talks, coupled with their body language assists in developing an impression of that person's character.

King James, I was another distinguished philosopher who was the initial investigator of facial gestures. His saying, "As the tongue speaketh to the ear so the gesture speaketh to the eye," speaks massively when influencing naysayers that facial expressions are indeed a silent language that speaks volumes when deciphered accurately.

Charles Darwin was also a philosopher who, like King James I, took a very special interest in the way people expressed emotions in their faces. Darwin is noted for performing one of the first research studies in determining how people distinguish emotion in their face. Darwin's belief was that facial muscles operated in unison to produce a few broad facial expressions. In order to test what he believed to be true, Darwin organized a study in which he displayed eleven random slides of individuals showing various facial expressions. The people who were participants in the study were to convey what emotion they felt the person in each picture slide exhibited.

Darwin's research ultimately concluded that in regards

to common emotions such as happiness, sadness, fear, and anger the results were unanimous and every respondent was in agreeance. Darwin went on to write a book in 1872 entitled, "*The Expressions of Emotions in Man and Animals*," which included the results of the facial expression study conducted.

CHAPTER 3: THE IMPORTANCE OF BODY LANGUAGE

Communication by body movement is commonly referred to as kinetics, and it happens to be a very important aspect of communication that many people actually forget about or tend to ignore, thinking that it has no significance. That couldn't be further from the truth. In all actuality, body language could, in some cases, seem to be stronger than words. We use it everywhere we go.

We can shrug our shoulders and, without a word, and we have just stated, "I don't have the foggiest idea." We can raise our eyebrows, and we've stated, "Excuse me? Did I hear you right?" We can hold our hands in front of us with palms up to the state, "I don't know what else to say. That is all I have." We can also use nose to indicate that the other individual "has it right!"

A portion of the things we say with our bodies can help us fortify why we are stating it. Just saying "I don't have the foggiest idea" has got nothing on including the accompanying motions. In the event that we hold our hands up over our face or in front of us as we raise our eyebrows and rearrange our grin while we stick our base lip marginally out and look to the side, more than likely will make somebody chuckle and maybe taken a touch of the weight of ourselves or the other individual who was somewhat apprehensive in a situation.

Many of the body language signals that we send are sent through our face. The face carries about 50 muscles, and the hue and moisture of it send many signals to the messenger. Surprisingly, not only the face sends various messages, so does the head and the direction that the head is positioned in also makes a bold statement about the way a person is feeling.

For example, the white skin may indicate that a person is intensely afraid or that the person is just could be very cold. A red face could mean that the person is extremely angry or that person could be hot. Sweating definitely indicates that someone is overexerted or it could also indicate fear and even a surge of excitement.

It would be wise to focus on the signs of body language as a whole and not so much individual behavior because it could become a little tricky. It would be wise to pay close attention to context clues, as well; these are huge indicators in deciphering feelings and emotions, and they also help set the tone of a conversation. The most universal facial expressions include happiness, sadness, anger, and confusion. The great philosopher, Charles Darwin proved this in many of his early research studies and Paul Ekman, a known analyst, has also concluded studies that support his theory.

Sometimes our body language doesn't align with the words that we speak. We may notice a lot with our children. You tell them to go clean up their room, they agree to do it, seemingly, without any issue but the look on their face may be one of aggravation or disdain, they may even roll their eyes or throw their hands up.

Or what about the children that don't want to eat their vegetables. They sit at the table for hours just eyeballing the food with a disgusted look on their little faces. You constantly reinforce eating their vegetables and they slowly and sluggishly retort, "OK," and with slumped shoulders and a pinched nose, they reluctantly gulp them done. I have very vivid memories of both of these repetitive occasions. The words just don't match up with the actions and for a good reason, in their minds.

Granted we are all human beings, and our actions won't match up with our words one hundred percent of the time. However, there are situations where body language and spoken word not matching up can hurt people and be downright toxic. This will be discussed in a later chapter. It is important to get to know and understand body language because it can decrease the chances of miscommunication and conflict. It also can help us discern friendships and romantic relationships, as well as, help us improve chances of being hired for a job. Whatever the case, being about to decode body language has positive impacts on both our personal and professional lives.

CHAPTER 4: UNDERSTANDING BODY LANGUAGE

BODY LANGUAGE ATTRACTION

Body language is a basic element of fascination. When we discuss love, dating, and sentiment, body language assumes a major part.

Such a large number of individuals ponder:

"What occurred in this relationship?"

"Do they like me?"

"Why didn't they call?"

Body language will give you the knowledge to know where you stand.

The question is how would we utilize body language to be alluring and how does body language assume a part in fascination?

It's pretty riveting to know that our cave dweller predecessors utilized a similar body language. However, that body language has been hugely expanded upon. Here are some messages we attempt to send with our body to show interest in another person:

- I'm open
- I'm innocuous

- I'm intrigued
- I'm congenial
- I'm prolific

The question is, how does fascination happen?

Rutgers University anthropologist Helen Fisher, says that the human body knows instantly in one moment whether somebody's physically alluring or not. Here are the body language signals that people generally find appealing:

• Availability: Both guys and females discover individuals with accessible body language the most appealing. Accessible body language is grinning, uncrossed arms, uncrossed legs and upward looking (not looking down at shoes or telephones).

• Fertility: From a transformative point of view, people are tuned into body language prompts that flag fruitfulness and youth. Fortunately, these can be underlined with body language. For men, standing up straight, squaring the shoulders, planting feet somewhat more than shoulder width separated and showing hands are all indications of fruitfulness. For a lady, holding your hair down, tilting your go to uncover pheromones and keeping hands and wrists obvious to show the delicate skin of the wrists are very alluring for men.

BODY LANGUAGE EYE CONTACT

Outward appearance is fundamental while communicating feelings through the body. Blends of eyes, eyebrow, lips, nose, and cheek developments help shape distinctive states of mind of an individual (e.g. upbeat, pitiful, discouraged, irate, and so forth.).

A couple thinks about to demonstrate that outward appearance and real expression (i.e. non-verbal communication) are consistent when deciphering feelings. Behavioral analyses have likewise demonstrated that acknowledgment of outward appearance is affected by seen real expression. This implies the cerebrum forms the others facial and substantial expressions all the while. Subjects in these reviews demonstrated exactness in judging feelings in light of outward appearance. This is on account of the face, and the body are ordinarily observed together in their regular extents, and the passionate signs from the face and body are very much coordinated.

BODY LANGUAGE OF LOVE

Do you ever wish there was an enchantment wand that would make you more appealing to the inverse sex, or if nothing else helps you comprehend who is pulled into you? All things considered, it's no enchantment yet a science. Here's the manner by which men and ladies can figure out how to ace the specialty of adoration.

"Body language is hardwired into our brains, and subsequently frequently utilized as a part of oblivious developments," says Allan Pease, non-verbal communication master and creator of The Body Language of Love, "Ladies are better wired for getting on non-verbal signs, so if men need to expand their odds in the mating diversion, then they ought to figure out how to translate signals ladies ordinarily utilize."

BODY LANGUAGE GESTURES

Motions are developments made with body parts (e.g. hands, arms, fingers, head, legs) and they might be willful or automatic. Arm signals can be deciphered in a few ways. In a discourse, when one stands, sits or even strolls with collapsed arms, this is typically not an inviting signal. It could imply that they have a shut personality and are in all probability unwilling to tune into the speaker's perspective. Another kind of arm motion additionally incorporates an arm traversed the other, showing instability and an absence of certainty.

Hand motions regularly imply the condition of the prosperity of the individual making them. Loose hands show certainty and confidence, while gripped hands might be translated as indications of stress or outrage. On the off chance that a man is wringing their hands, this exhibits apprehension and uneasiness.

Finger signals are additionally generally used to epitomize one's discourse and in addition, mean the condition of the prosperity of the individual making them. In specific societies, guiding utilizing one's pointer is considered worthy. Be that as it may, indicating at a man might be seen as forceful in different societies—for instance, individuals who share Hindu convictions consider blame is dealing hostile. Rather, they point with their thumbs. In like manner, the thumbs up signal could demonstrate "alright" or "great" in nations like the US, France, and Germany. In any case, this same signal is offending in different nations like Iran, Bangladesh, and Thailand, where it is what might as well be called demonstrating the center finger in the US.

In many societies, the Head Nod is utilized to mean "Yes" or understanding. It's a hindered type of bowing - the individual typically goes to bow, however, holds back, bringing about the gesture. Bowing is an easygoing signal, so the Head Nod indicates we are obliging the other individual's perspective. Look into directed with individuals who were conceived hard of hearing, idiotic and visually impaired demonstrates that they likewise utilize this motion to imply 'Yes,' so it gives off an impression of being an inalienable signal of accommodation.

FLIRTING BODY LANGUAGE
The principle component of being a tease, body language is stressing sexual contrasts; highlighting

these distinctions is the thing that makes a man attractive to other individuals. As indicated by Dr. Albert Scheflen, when a man meets somebody they are occupied with, certain physiological changes occur.

The muscle tone expands, body listing vanishes, the body expect erect stance, and the individual seems more youthful and more appealing.

A man will stand taller, extend his trunk and look all the more intense and overwhelming, while the lady will tilt her head, and touch her hair while uncovering her wrists. Body language uncovers how accessible, appealing, energetic or even how edgy we are.

A few signs of being a tease Body language are oblivious and totally characteristic, while different signs are examined and purposeful; in any case, the center standard of being a tease Body language is underlining sexual contrasts so as to draw in the inverse sex. Highlighting these distinctions is the thing that makes a man look and feels "provocative."

Various reviews into romance demonstrated that ladies are initiators of a sentimental experience 90% of the time. They do it by sending unpretentious signs – eye, face and body flags that are sent to their male counterpart.

On the off chance that a man was sufficiently discerning to decipher the signs, he would, for the most part, approach them. While a few men approach even with no signs being sent to them, their general achievement rate with romances is low, since they are drawn closer to women when they are not welcome. Surprisingly, while it may seem as if men are the ones who mainly make the first move, in 90% of experiences, that is not the case.

In all actuality, men are bad at receiving and effectively translating inconspicuous signs of the female body language, particularly in the event that it was exceptionally unobtrusive. They have about 10 to 20 times more testosterone than ladies, and they may mix up neighborly grins with sexual intrigue.

Notwithstanding that, numerous women get a kick out of the chance to send negating signals when they are, indeed, intrigued. This action actually allows them an opportunity to assess the man. Because of this clashing data, a few men will get befuddled and won't make their approach by any means, paying little mind to what signs are being conveyed.

POSITIVE BODY LANGUAGE

When I discuss positive body language, I mean open, intrigued and congenial, as opposed to the inverse, guarded body language we talked about previously. This doesn't mean that it is the "best" body language you ought to dependably utilize, yet rather a bunch of signs that transmit a liberal and cordial state of mind.

This obviously can be something to be thankful for, so how about we see what we can do to make others "open up" to us and set up trust by demonstrating consideration and ability to collaborate.

KEEP AWAY FROM BARRIERS

So as to set up trust with anybody, we have to demonstrate to them that we're not a risk to them and that we don't fear them either. Keep in mind that protective body language influences our mentality, so in case we're on edge, it would be hard for others to approach us and for us to acknowledge them.

Warming up to someone is clearly a procedure; don't be surprised if a person doesn't immediately "open up" to you at your first advance. In the event that the other person does show interest, you can speed up the "warming up" process, or if nothing else, comprehend their general demeanor towards you.

When you first meet someone expect the crossed body position with their arms and legs, and they will most likely, keep an extensive separation from each other. Then closing their jacket also shows a sign of unfamiliarity or discomfort. As the relations warm up, the leg boundary will vanish, and they may begin to get closer to you.

Next, they will begin to motion increasingly and uncover their palms. After that, the arms may come uncrossed, which is a good indication that the person is becoming more comfortable. Watch for the person's body to begin to incline and lean in toward yours; this is also a good sign.

We intuitively duplicate the body language of others around us. You can likewise invert the procedure by accepting a cautious position yourself. This procedure relies solely relies upon the unique circumstance (a fun party versus an arbitrary meeting between total outsiders in the city), the character (contemplative person versus outgoing person) and the way of life.

Keeping away from hindrances is the initial phase in anticipating positive body language, you wipe out the impediments, this is the ideal opportunity to show genuineness and trust the stuff that assembled great long haul connections.

Do you recall the way your relative or companion welcomed you home after a long flight? They presumably spread their arms upwards and uncovered their palms, as if they were grasping you from a remote place. This exceptionally open and positive motion truly warms the heart.

All things considered, while you can't utilize this positioning in the circumstances with EVERYONE. Had your supervisor seen this position, they may speculate that you possibly won the lottery or that your brain took some time off, yet you can utilize comparative signals to venture open, fair and positive body language.

The method of keeping your palms uncovered shows readiness genuineness, and that you have nothing to cover up. It indicates you can be trusted. Different signs that can help you anticipate earnestness and collaboration are:

• Keeping your body straight – to venture certainty and vitality.

• Keeping great eye contact – demonstrates that you are mindful and unafraid.

• Keeping your head in impartial position – don't bow to them yet don't look down on them either.

• Keeping your body and garments open and abstain from holding objects before you.

• Smile.

When you like somebody you need to get closer to them, it's that simple. The closer you get, the more intrigued you are. Subsequently, inclining forward, particularly when joined with gesturing and grinning, is the most unmistakable approach to state non-verbally: "yes, I like what you're stating, continue onward."

Does it imply that you ought to constantly incline and gesture?

Obviously not. Trying too hard prompts two fundamental issues:

1. By overextending your incline, you can coincidentally attack individual space and make distress for the other individual. That is likewise the motivation behind why we incline forward when we attempt to threaten our rival, just this kind of incline is much tenser and forceful.

2. On the off chance that you gesture, grin and incline constantly, with all individuals, you will dependably seem anxious to if it's not too much trouble and in this manner, you bring down your status according to others.

Consider inclining as driving, the more you push on the gas, the more drew in, and enthusiastic you are and the less you push – the more casual and far off you are. So you don't need a slip to the limits, and you generally need to interchange your "speed" to coordinate the circumstance.

Furthermore, much the same as in driving, the course of the incline has essentials. We subliminally incline and motion towards the spots or things we need.

BODY LANGUAGE COMMUNICATION

Feelings can likewise be identified through body stances. Look into has demonstrated that body stances are all the more precisely perceived when a feeling is contrasted and an alternate or unbiased feeling. For instance, a man feeling irate would depict strength over the other, and their stance would show approach inclinations. Contrasting this with a man feeling dreadful: they would feel feeble, docile and their stance would show shirking propensities, the inverse of a furious individual.

Sitting or standing stances additionally demonstrate one's feelings. A man sitting till the back of their seat inclines forward with their head gesturing alongside the discourse infers that they are open, loose and by and large prepared to tune in. Then again, a man who has their legs and arms crossed with the foot kicking marginally suggests that they are feeling eager and candidly disengaged from the exchange.

In a standing exchange, a man remains with arms akimbo with feet pointed towards the speaker could propose that they are mindful and is keen on the discussion. Be that as it may, a little distinction in this stance could mean a great deal. Remaining with arms akimbo is viewed as discourteous in Bali.

Open and sweeping nonverbal posing can likewise effectively affect testosterone and cortisol levels, which have clear ramifications for the investigation of human conduct

CONFIDENT BODY LANGUAGE

How do a few people seem certain, while others appear to be uncertain or on edge in some ways? On the off chance that you can motivate others to think you are certain, then they may well trust and trust you all the more effectively. Interestingly, in the event that you seem indeterminate, how might they acknowledge what you say as being valid?

Still

Restless individuals are tense, and it appears. Their bodies are continually moving, normally in jerky developments that double-cross their strong pressure.

Standing

At the point when a restless individual is standing, they normally get 'cheerful feet,' venturing around the place.

A certain individual is open to remaining in one place, without tapping their feet.

Adjust your weight equitably, with feet fixed a hip-width separated. At the point when weight is on one leg, it demonstrates status to move. When you are adjusted, you are immovably planted, showing goal to stay and having no dread of assault.

Sitting

When sitting, put yourself easily, reclining in the seat instead of tensely forward. You may put your hands on your lap or behind your head when unwinding, or steeple them when settling on evaluative choices.

Keep the lower body still, with both feet fixed on the ground or inexactly crossed for solace. Weaved or jerking legs are indications of uneasiness.

Head

One of the least complex approaches to show certainty is to keep your head still. On edge, individuals are continually searching for dangers. Settle on a point before you to help you keep your head in one place.

Keep your head upright and with your button level, as though you were suspended from a point at the crown of your head. On edge, individuals tend to hold the button low, initially with a specific end goal to shield the helpless neck from assault.

Arms

We frequently wave our arms about when talking or fasten them together when concerned. While you can make littler developments, by and large, you can permit them to stay composed, resting in your lap or hanging next to you. A certain typical posture with hands is held daintily in front or behind the back (this is run of the mill of sovereignty and presidents). Holding one's own particular hands can be viewed as an indication of nervousness so do be watchful with this.

Wriggling is an indication of nervousness. Sure individuals can keep their hands still without the need to move or shroud them. Demonstrating one's hands is a method for building certainty as it shows you are not skittish, have no weapons nor are balling clench hands. Consequently, it is a smart thought to keep your hands out of any pockets, in spite of the fact that thumbs delicately in pockets can demonstrate an easygoing certainty.

CHAPTER 5: BODY LANGUAGE IN THE WORKPLACE

Body language has various positive impacts when used correctly in the workplace. Some advantages include helping to motivate coworkers, increase productivity, help build better relationships and bonds, and help you to be more confident and poised. Here are a few pointers on how to own your position and gain the proper respect that you deserve.

- **Maintain eye contact**. This exudes confidence, power, and an undeniable trust factor. Make your eye contact engage and assure that you are actively listening when you are in conversation. Occasionally look away when in conversation, you don't want it to get weird or awkward, however, when making the eye contact shift your eyes slowly from left to right while conversing to confirm you are paying attention to the speaker.

- **Try a Power Pose.** Studies have been conducted through Harvard and Columbia

Business Schools that indicate putting your body in a "high-power" pose for a couple of minutes work wonders for building your confidence level. You basically adopt the pose of a powerful person, in the pose you are taking up a lot of space and the arms and legs are a significant distance from the body, i.e. a reclining position with your legs propped up on a desk or chest poked out and hands placed on your hips.

- **Put on a smile**. We sometimes get so consumed with dealing with the stresses of life that we forget to smile. You have to leave the worry and stress at home and come to work a different person, so to speak. Smiling indicates that you are a happy, friendly, welcoming, and helpful individual. People will be more prone to approaching you and engaging with you.

- **Keep them arms unfolded.** We have a tendency to fold our arms when we don't know what else to do with them. This isn't a good move because it puts you in a defensive stance and implies that you are being introverted and trying to block out the outside world. Crossing your arms alludes to you feeling unconfident and awkward at that moment.

- **Speak with your hands.** I know we have been taught to not talk with our hands and have been reminded on numerous occasions how annoying it can be, however, studies have shown that speaking with your hands actually helps to organize your thoughts, think more clearly, and decrease the usage of filler words. Furthermore, people who talk with their hands are regarded as being pleasant, warm, and lively.

SMALL GROUP SITUATIONS

Focusing on an associate or subordinate's body language can help you decide how to continue. In a one-on-one or little gathering circumstance, taking note of body language helps you reveal an absence of certainty, an issue in a present venture or even contemptible from a worker. By properly assessing body language, you can distinguish potential issues and discover answers for them.

In the event that a representative doesn't feel certain about a specific assignment, extra preparing or support is recommended. On the off chance that you sense that an issue with a venture happened, you can work to take care of the issue. Body language can uncover more than your representatives will let you know with their words so you can better maintain the working environment.

In a kinship, one's body language can show that somebody is focusing or doesn't generally think about what the other individual is stating. Inclining forward into the discussion shows that this individual is occupied with hearing what the other individual is stating. Reclining would show that he was unbiased or felt himself unrivaled. Inclining forward and standing close while talking may demonstrate that somebody is forcefully attempting to convince the other individual or attempting to rule the discussion. Tuning into somebody while not looking demonstrates that you are not by any stretch of the imagination focusing, yet just sitting tight for your opportunity to talk. This gives your companion the inclination that you aren't generally thinking about them and what they need to state. This is downright rude!

GATHERINGS OR PRESENTATIONS

When giving an introduction or driving a meeting, you can gauge the body language of your audience in order to access how your message was taken. Your audience may feel exhausted or separated in the event that they maintain a strategic distance from eye contact, squirm with items, for example, pens or notepads, jot or have poor posture. Coworkers or superiors who feel cautious or who can't help contradicting your message will probably move in the opposite direction of you, keep their arms crossed or evade eye contact. If the staff appears to differ with your message, you can open up the dialog to address the issue and concoct arrangements together.

Positive Approach

Negative Approach

JOB INTERVIEW

In the meeting room, it's ok to put a thin portfolio on the table, particularly in the event that you'll be showing its substance, however, put other possessions on the floor alongside you. Holding a folder case or satchel on your lap will make you appear as if you're attempting to make a hindrance around yourself, alerts Craig.

Abstain from inclining forward, which makes you seem to shut off, Bowden says. Rather, he exhorts sitting up straight and showing your neck, trunk and stomach zone - to flag that you're open.
When motioning with your hands, Craig says, you ought to dependably keep them over the work area and underneath the collarbone. "Any higher will seem berserk," she says.

Bowden prompts that you keep your hands even lower, in what he calls "reality plane" - a zone that fans out 180 degrees from your navel. "Motioning from here imparts that you're focused, controlled and quiet - and that you need to help," he says.

It's fine to sit about a foot far from the table so that your signals are unmistakable, he says.

Body language could be the deciding variable in a prospective employee meet-up. On the off chance that the candidate's body language states that he is comfortable with the topic and passes on certainty, he has a higher likelihood of landing the position.

CHAPTER 6: THE PSYCHOLOGY OF BODY LANGUAGE

Individuals are always diverting from a tempest of signs. These signs may be (non-verbal) messages imparted through the sender's body developments, outward appearances, voice tone and clamor. I'm pretty sure you have heard the old saying, "Fake it until you make it" more than a handful of times, but how many actually know that the science behind the saying has plenty of truth to it?

There have been various studies that have proved the saying to be true to its word. Researcher Fritz Strack conducted a double-blind study where he told one group of people to put a pen between their lips, and the other group put a pen between their teeth.

The group with the pen between their teeth resembled smiling people and the ones with the pen between their lips looked as if they were frowning. All of the participants were presented with some funny material to read, and the group with the pen between their lips didn't think that the material was as funny as the group with the pen between their teeth. This study proved that the facial expression that you represent on the outside, whether it's forced or genuine, has the ability to affect your mental state.

It's always a good thing to be aware of your emotions and what you convey to the world, so, rather than utilizing your telephone just to catch recordings of adorable pet traps to post on YouTube, put it on you and record yourself doing normal everyday tasks. You'll have the capacity to see and analyze the dialect signals that you pass on excessively, too little, or simply the wrong message about how you're feeling. Partner up with a companion or loved one and audit the recordings, searching for the signals that you most need to take work on or adjust.

Guiding analyst and previous University of Massachusetts teacher, Alan Ivey spearheaded the technique for micro-training in order to help instructors enhance the way they convey to their clientele. In order to profit the most from this sort of re-instruction of body language, prepare to practice it in a non-basic or judgmental form. Your body's activities, deliberately and unwittingly, mirror your mental state. Figuring out how to control the signals you impart to others will perpetually help the way you look, as well as the way you feel.

CHAPTER 7: BODY LANGUAGE OF A FLIRTING WOMAN

Here's the good stuff! This is what you've been anticipating because everybody and their cousin is looking for love and has that one main woman/man that they've been crushing on. You've been wondering if that person feels the same about you but of course asking them is nowhere in the question. What if they don't feel the same way about you?

You would look like a complete creeper! (Gasp) Well, let's get right down to learning how to read that body language, so you won't look like the love obsessed creeper that you really are! Just kidding, a little humor goes a long way, especially when dealing with matters of the heart. At the point when ladies feel pulled into you, they are normally to a great degree unobtrusive. Be it as it may, some are coyer and will purposefully attempt to pass on signs that she is intrigued. Here are signs that a lady is potentially showing interest in you through her body language.

1). **Pay attention to her feet**. I know it sounds

kind of weird, but the feet can determine attitude. If her feet are pointed toward you, she's showing that she's attracted to you. If they are pointed away from you, not so much.

2). **She touches you**. Whether she grabs your hand during a conversation, purposely bumps you, or taps you playfully. This subtle "love tap" interaction indicates that she feels comfortable with you and she may touch you many times while you are together, this is a huge hint that's she is into you.

3). **She gets nerves**. Women sometimes also may show signs of nervousness when they are attracted to someone. Actions such as playing with her watch, chewing her gum super-fast, messing around with her phone, or her jewelry are all signs that she is nervous or maybe even little shy. If she purposefully does these things as she converses with you, she's attempting to uncover parts of her body that discharge pheromones. Your opinion of her is very much a major concern if she is attracted to you. You not feeling the same way about her could do some damage to her self-esteem and morale. Purposefully does these things as she converses with you, she's attempting to uncover parts of her body that discharge pheromones.

4). **Focus in on her legs**. Women who are interested in you will usually cross their legs and similarly to feet, her top leg will be pointed in your direction. It this case, you know you've got her attention, and she is attracted. If she happens to use her hands to stroke or tap on her legs, she is trying to draw attention to them.

5). **Being a copycat**. If she happens to mirror every move that you make, it's not that she's trying to be annoying; she's just flirting with you! More than likely she is not even aware of the synchronous behavior because it feels so natural. She is basically non-verbally stating that she understands you and feels the same way you do.

So, how about if she's not that into you? Here are a couple of indicators to keep an eye out for:

- **The eyes tell no lies**. If a woman is blatantly avoiding eye contact with you especially if she knows you are looking at her that usually indicates she's not interested. If a woman is interested, she tends to try to hold eye contact with you and if broken the eye contact is quickly picked back up. If you are in a conversation with her and realize that her eyes are everywhere else and not focused in on yours, she has tuned out of the conversation and is extremely bored and trying to figure how to politely exit stage left.

- **The use of closed body language**. Someone who is interested tends to use more open body language, such as pointing their body in your direction or sitting in a more upright position. However, closed body language may be something like crossing her arms, putting a purse between you guys, or slouching in a chair. Those actions imply a disinterest, and she's trying to isolate herself from you, inadvertently indicating that she doesn't want you to invade her space.

- **Mouthing off**. So, here the mouth can be very revealing. If you hold a conversation with her and her disposition shows distaste and in this case, pay attention to her mouth because at this moment if you notice that she is pulling a corner of her mouth back, it's an indicator that she's not interested in you at all.

There are numerous strategies that a lady will use when taking a gander at somebody she prefers. At the point when a lady raises her eyebrows, while in the meantime bringing down her eyelids, she is reproducing an outward appearance of delight. Different expressions incorporate, yet not constrain to quickly flickering and holding eye contact, holding eye contact and grinning or smiling or licking her lips. In the event that a young lady is timid, you may catch her staring or grinning at you when you're not looking.

Being the not-so-detail oriented beings that we sometimes are known to be, men often times can miss blatant signals that a female is interested in them. According to researcher Monika Moore, men often miss a women's first courtship signal. On average women need to eye-gaze three times before a man takes notice. Keep in mind the old saying that actions speak louder than words and pay close attention to those signs that she is throwing, fellows. The woman that you are dating now could potentially be the woman that you marry later.

CHAPTER 8: BODY LANGUAGE SIGNS THAT HE LIKES YOU

Ladies, there is a near absence of male romance signs. "Men don't play a romance amusement," says Barbara. "They just react to it." Consequently men maybe a tad bit easier than women to figure out because they are the "say what you mean and mean what you say" types, whereas, women who are the "I said it but my mind can be altered depending on the way the wind blows" types. *I hope you are catching what I'm throwing here!* Without further ado, here are a couple of foolproof ways to tell that he really likes you.

1). **He gives you a real smile.** I'm not talking about one of those half-hearted grins. I'm talking a full, teeth showing, genuine smile like he's just won a million bucks. His smile must engage his entire face, that's when you know that he's having a good time and is feeling your vibe. If he just gives you a subtle grin, it suggests that he's putting on a front.

2). **Throat touching.** Being that the throat is the

origin for conversation, his touching it indicates that he's concerned about making a good impression on you. Interestingly enough, the touch or rubbing the neck area also can express a sense of uneasiness or self-doubt.

3). **Hand motions.** When he offers to hold your hand, and you notice that his palms are facing up, this is a clear indication that he is into you. The crossing of the fingers is another little tactic that is used to show that he wants to bond with you and is interested in knowing you better.

4). **The hair fiddle.** Whether he is rubbing his hands through it, slicking it back, or just trying to touch it up, it is a huge indicator that he is showing interest. He could also perform this act out of nervousness or out of routine; however, it still shows an intense passion.

5). **Catch a sneak peak of the way he stands.** While this can be done subconsciously, men often time will stand with the feet apart and planted firmly on the ground as to indicate that they aren't going anywhere, and they tend to poke out their chest to put their masculinity on display and give off that dominant, macho kind of vibe that women seem to gravitate toward.

Here is a couple of signs that clearly pinpoint when it's time to request that check a little earlier than planned.

- **Nose touching.** It may appear as though he's trying to slyly try to pick away a booger but that may not be the case here. This slick action means that something adverse is going on or in his thought process and it is also could mean that he's lying to you.

- **Play his position.** If he stands far away from you and maintains a distance from you throughout the date, this is not a good sign. Try leaning into him and attempt to get closer to him, if he backs off, then he's definitely not interested. Some men could seem to be a little standoffish because they don't want to appear to come on too strong or they could just be more reserved.

- **Hidden hands.** If your guy keeps his hands in his pocket or barely shows his hands when he is around you, it means that he's not comfortable around you or simply not interested. An interested and comfortable person tends to make hand gestures when they are communicating with another person.

OTHER BODY LANGUAGE TO TAKE NOTE OF

- Jiggling feet is an indication of fatigue.
- Locked lower legs indicate negative feelings.
- Extended flickering, covering their mouth, rubbing eyes all mean the individual is lying.
- When a man is wearing tight-fitting pants such as, a small size Speedos or dangling the long end of a belt or a pack of keys before their groin, it means they're putting their manliness in plain view. It's the same as a lady with a push-up bra.
- When a man mirrors a lady's outward appearances, she'll think he is minding and appealing.
- A marginally astonished, curious expression implies he discovers you captivating

Please be mindful that these hints are just that. Every person is different and has their own specific set of characteristics; no two people alike so keep that in mind when trying to read people's body language. Be aware of context clues and take them into consideration before attempting to figure out what is it is that a person's body language is conveying. Often times, mixed signals are thrown in, and you have to look at the big picture as opposed to individual body movements.

CONCLUSION

Body language plays a very important role in our everyday lives. Without it, it would be difficult to decipher the real meaning behind people's words and attitudes. As we have learned there are many avenues and aspects of body language that need to be considered when attempting to decode what a person is trying to convey. Keep in mind that facial expressions, eye movement, perspiration, and even breathing all are considered to be forms of body language.

Honestly, normally these factors are ignored or taken for granted because they are so "natural" to human beings and being that it's so commonplace for people to engage their bodies in conversation, it's easy to overlook it. However, people who pay attention to body language really do have an advantage over those who don't even notice it. People who are intelligent enough to pay attention or listen to other people's body language usually are people who have a keen sense of their environments, and the benefits include being able to determine when someone is a danger to you or others, determine when others need help, or special attention or affection.

Being that I watch a lot of crime and investigation television shows, a person with a heightened sense of surroundings and awareness would make a great star witness to a crime because that person would be able to tell authorities everything that they need to know about a potential suspect – from what color shoes they were wearing to the tattoos they may have had on their bodies.

It is important to study body language in order to better understand a person and become more relatable, however, it is also just as important not to put too much emphasize on body language alone because it can definitely be rather deceiving. A person's words don't always add up what their body language is saying, and yes, this actually does often happening, usually subconsciously. That is why it is wise to assure that you focus in on context clues and make sure you obtain all the details of a conversation, not just some of it or the juicy portion.

REFERENCES

1. Klima, Edward S.; & Bellugi, Ursula. (1979). The signs of language. Cambridge, MA: Harvard University Press. ISBN 0-674-80795-2.

2. Sandler, Wendy; & Lillo-Martin, Diane. (2006). Sign Language and Linguistic Universals. Cambridge: Cambridge University Press.

3. Barfield, T (1997). The dictionary of anthropology. Illinois: Blackwell Publishing.

4. Onsager, Mark. "Understanding the Importance of Non-Verbal Communication"], Body Language Dictionary, New York, 19 May 2014. Retrieved on 26 October 2014.

5. Kurien, Daisy N (March 1, 2010). "Body Language: Silent Communicator at the Workplace." IUP Journal of Soft Skills. 4 (1/2): 29–36.

6. Gu, Yuanyuan; Mai, Xiaoqin; Luo, Yue-jia; Di Russo, Francesco (23 July 2013). "Do Bodily Expressions Compete with Facial

Expressions? Time Course of Integration of Emotional Signals from the Face and the Body". PLoS ONE. 8 (7): e66762. doi:10.1371/journal.pone.0066762.

7.   Kret, ME; Pichon, S; Grezes, J; de Gelder, B (Jan 15, 2011). "Similarities and differences in perceiving a threat from dynamic faces and bodies. An fMRI study". NEUROIMAGE. 54 (2): 1755–1762. doi:10.1016/j.neuroimage.2010.08.012. PMID 20723605.

8.   Edwards, V. (2013). Male Body Language. The science of People.

www.ingramcontent.com/pod-product-compliance
Lightning Source LLC
Chambersburg PA
CBHW071248280526
45788CB00004B/1623